Fathers

are
Forever

Dr. Criswell Freeman

Fathers

are
Forever

Dr. Criswell Freeman

Simon & Schuster, Inc.
New York London Toronto Sydney

Simon & Schuster, Inc.
1230 Avenue of the Americas, New York, New York 10020

Scripture quotations are taken from:

Scriptures marked NIV® are from the *Holy Bible, New International Version®*. Copyright © 1973, 1978, 1984 by International Bible Society. Used by permission of Zondervan Publishing House. All rights reserved.

Scriptures marked KJV are taken from the *Holy Bible, King James Version*.

Cover Design & Page Layout by Bart Dawson

Manufactured in the United States of America

10 9 8 7 6 5 4 3 2 1

ISBN-13: 978-1-4169-2570-5
ISBN-10: 1-4169-2570-8

For Dad

Table of Contents

Introduction

Y ou hold in your hands a simple tribute to fathers.

On these pages, you will examine the attributes of dynamic dads and peerless pops. You will consider the skills of fabulous fathers and great granddads. And, you will discover a heaping helping of fatherly advice.

This collection of quotations celebrates the paternal side of parenting, and with good cause. Fathers bequeath a timeless legacy—one that is passed from generation to generation. The hand that rocks the cradle also places its handprint upon eternity. A father's love lasts a lifetime—and beyond.

If you happen to be a father, and since you're reading this book there is a high probability that you are, congratulations and thank you. In touching the lives of your children and their friends, you have left the world a better place. Your handiwork will endure...forever.

Chapter 1
A Father Is...

No music is so
pleasant to my ears
as that word—
father.

—

Lydia Maria Child

The dictionary defines father as "a male parent," but every grateful son or daughter knows that such a concise definition is woefully incomplete. A good father is many things: He is a leader, a provider, an advisor, a disciplinarian, a teacher, a coach, a recreation director, a friend, a spiritual guide, a baby-sitter, a transportation director, a handyman, a physician, and a banker.

To a young child, a father is an all-purpose, all-powerful, all-knowing figure. As the child matures and the teenage years reach full bloom, the father's image may become tarnished—temporarily. But, the adult child, armed with a better understanding of the demands of parenthood, is likely to appreciate his or her father more than ever. And rightly so.

On the pages that follow, we consider the wide-ranging implications of fatherhood, a job so demanding and so important that God reserved it for that great fraternity of homeplace heroes: our dads.

There is no more vital calling or vocation
for men than fathering.

—John R. Throop

A father is the man who expects his son
to be as good as the man he meant to be.

—Franklin A. Clark

One father equals a hundred schoolmasters.

—George Herbert

A father provides love, strength, wisdom,
security, example, friendship, and fun.

—Jim Gallery

Children's children are the crown of
old men; the glory of children
are their fathers.

—Proverbs 17:6 KJV

Tell me who your father is and
I'll tell you who you are.

—Philippine Proverb

You are a king by your own fireside,
    as much as any monarch in his thrown.
                        ——Miguel de Cervantes

A father is a banker provided by nature.
                        ——French Proverb

The most important thing a father can do
    for his children is to love their mother.
                        ——Rev. Theodore M. Hesburgh

A father is a man who can't get on
        the phone, in the bathroom,
        or out of the house.
                        ——Anonymous

Raising Our Children

Every child is a priceless gift from the Father above. With that gift comes immense responsibility. Wise parents understand the critical importance of raising their children with love, with family, with discipline, and with faith.

It has been said, quite correctly, that our children are on loan from God. It might be added that the term of that loan is all too brief. In the blink of an eye—or so it seems—our babies are grown and gone. Thus, each day that we spend with our children is indeed a gift...but a gift with a definite time limit. May we, as parents, use that time wisely.

Have we not all one father? Did not one God create us?

—

Malachi 2:10 NIV

Chapter 2
Family

A happy family is but an earlier heaven.

—

Sir John Bowring

Sam Levenson joked, "Insanity is hereditary, you can get it from your kids." Spoken like a man with a big family.

An anonymous parent once observed, "A loving family is a thing of beauty and a job forever." Unfortunately, this statement is only partially true. Parenting is, of course, a job, but the work of raising our children is not "forever"; it is temporary. Still, we can be comforted in the knowledge that the fruits of our parental labors, our children (and their children), outlive us just as surely as our children influence the world in ways that we can never fully comprehend.

The philosopher George Santayana wrote, "A family is a masterpiece of nature." In this chapter, we consider that masterpiece...and its master, dear old Dad.

A family is a place where principles are
hammered and honed on the anvil
of everyday living.

—Charles R. Swindoll

A home is a place where we find direction.

—Gigi Graham Tchividjian

Money can build or buy a house.
Add love to that, and you have a home.
Add God to that, and you have a temple.

—Anne Ortland

No man can possibly know what life
means, what the world means,
what anything means,
until he has a child and loves it.

—Lafcadio Hearn

Other things may change us, but we start
and end with the family.

—Anthony Brandt

Upon our children—how they are taught—
rests the fate, or fortune,
of tomorrow's world.

—B. C. Forbes

A family is a unit composed not only of
children, but of men, women, an occasional
animal, and the common cold.

—Ogden Nash

It takes a heap of lovin' in a house to make it
a home.

—Edgar A. Guest

You don't choose your family.
        They are God's gift to you,
            as you are to them.

—Desmond Tutu

There are three partners in any man:
        God, his father, and his mother.

—Old Saying

Blessed indeed is the man who hears many
        gentle voices call him father!

—Lydia Maria Child

A child is the greatest poem ever known.

—Christopher Morley

A family is the first and essential cell
of human society.

—Pope John XXIII

When the family is together,
the soul is at peace.

—Russian Proverb

A family is the school of duties founded
on love.

—Felix Adler

A large family gives beauty to the house.

—Indian Proverb

A family divided against itself will
perish together.

—Indian Proverb

The family you come from isn't as
important as the family
you're going to have.

—Ring Lardner

Father and mother are the most precious
jewels on earth.

—Philippine Proverb

Children have more need of models
than critics.

—Joseph Joubert

The family is the nucleus of civilization.

—Will and Ariel Durant

Lucky is that man whose children make
his happiness in life.

—Euripides

Creating a warm, caring, supportive,
encouraging environment is probably
the most important thing
you can do for your family.

—Stephen Covey

A baby is God's opinion that
the world should go on.

—Carl Sandburg

A child is a beam of sunlight from
the Infinite and Eternal.

—Lyman Abbott

A torn jacket is soon mended,
but hard words bruise the heart of a child.

—Henry Wadsworth Longfellow

It is a wise father that knows his own child.
—William Shakespeare

A father's interest in having a child—
perhaps his only child—may be unmatched
by any other interest in his life.
—William H. Rehnquist

About his children every parent is blind.
—Old Saying

Build me a son, O Lord, who will be
strong enough to know when he is weak
and brave enough to face himself
when he is afraid.
—Douglas MacArthur

We can either grace our children,
  or damn them with unrequited wounds
    which never seem to heal.
  Men, as fathers, you have such power.
                              —R. Kent Hughes

They say the best product off a farm
          is the children.
                              —Earl Simpson

All children alarm their parents,
      if only because you are forever
      expecting to encounter yourself.
                              —Gore Vidal

When a father helps a son, both smile;
  when a son must help his father, both cry.
                              —Old Jewish Saying

What we desire our children to become,
we must endeavor to be before them.

—Andrew Combe

A good father will leave his imprint
on his daughter for the rest of her life.

—James C. Dobson

When brothers agree, no fortress is
so strong as their common life.

—Antisthenes

In a big family, the first child is kind of like
the first pancake. If it's not perfect,
that's okay, there are a lot more
coming along.

—Antonin Scalia

The debt of gratitude we owe our mother
and father goes forward, not backward.
What we owe our parents is the bill presented
to us by our children.

—Nancy Friday

The voice of parents is the voice of gods,
for to their children they are
heaven's lieutenants.

—William Shakespeare

There is no grandfather who does not
adore his grandson.

—Victor Hugo

The father in praising the son
extols himself.

—Chinese Proverb

Your Family:
A Priceless Gift

Your most prized earthly possession is not your home, your car, or your savings account. Your most prized earthly possession is, of course, your family. Your family is a priceless gift from heaven above: treasure it, protect it, support it, and, above all, love it.

As a father, your responsibilities are profound; so are your rewards. Today and every day, give thanks for your clan, and then demonstrate your gratitude by serving up a heaping helping of laughter and leadership. Each day with your family is another blessing from God. Treasure the gift.

Home is the place where the great are small and the small are great.

—

Robert Savage

Chapter 3
Fatherly Advice

Whoever teaches his
son teaches not only
his son but also
his son's son.

—

The Talmud

A hundred years before the birth of Christ, Publilius Syrus observed, "Many receive advice, few profit from it." For twenty-one centuries, fathers everywhere have known exactly how he felt.

In a 1955 television interview, Harry Truman commented, "I have always found the best way to give advice to your children is to find out what they want and then advise them to do it." Obviously, President Truman spoke from experience. No matter how sound a father's recommendations may be, almost every child seems compelled to do it "my way."

In this chapter, we consider an assortment of helpful hints that fathers everywhere might be proud to share—and kids everywhere might be likely to ignore.

In our family, we try to make something
happen rather than wait around
for it to happen.
—James Jordan, Michael Jordan's father

My father is the standard by which all
subsequent men in my life have been judged.
—Kathryn McCarthy Graham

Advice is a sacred thing.
—Plato

We may give advice, but we cannot
inspire conduct.
—La Rochefoucauld

My son, hear the instruction of thy father.

—Proverbs 1:8 KJV

No one wants advice—only corroboration.

—John Steinbeck

Every morning at our house we had squats
and sit-ups 15 minutes before breakfast.
My father used to say,
"First you have to earn your breakfast."

—Arnold Schwarzenegger

The only thing Dad ever told me was to
go out and have fun, stay out of trouble,
and be a good kid.

—Ken Griffey, Jr.

Bitterness imprisons life, love releases it.

—Harry Emerson Fosdick

Scatter seeds of kindness.

—George Ade

No act of kindness, no matter how small,
is ever wasted.

—Aesop

Look upon the errors of others in sorrow,
not in anger.

—Henry Wadsworth Longfellow

Life is an exercise in forgiveness.

—Norman Cousins

The jealous are troublesome to others but
a torment to themselves.

—William Penn

Jealousy is a mental cancer.

—B. C. Forbes

Don't lose faith in humanity:
Think of all the people in
the United States who have never played
you a single nasty trick.

—Elbert Hubbard

The only way to have a friend is to be one.

—Ralph Waldo Emerson

If you can't stand yourself,
neither can anybody else!

—Sid Caesar

People ought to do what comes easy
 for them. Too many struggle with things
that are difficult for them and that they have
 no business trying to do.
—George Bernard Shaw

Work is a grand cure of all the maladies
 that ever beset mankind.
—Thomas Carlyle

Blessed is the man who has found his work.
—Elbert Hubbard

People who suffer in unsatisfying jobs are
 assuming the victim role. Nothing is going
to help them if they don't help themselves.
—Bernie Siegel, M.D.

Work and save.

—Bernard Baruch

If there is no wind, row.

—Latin Proverb

A gentleman never insults anyone
intentionally. Don't look for trouble,
but if you get into a fight,
make sure you win it.

—Clyde Morrison, John Wayne's Father

The secret of a long life is double careers.
One to about age 60, then another for
the next 30 years.

—David Ogilvy

Work as if you were to live 100 years;
pray as if you were to die tomorrow.

Ben Franklin

When you're green,
you're growing.
When you're ripe,
you rot.

—

Ray Kroc, the "Father"
of McDonald's Restaurants

Be slow in choosing a friend, slower in
changing a friendship.
—Benjamin Franklin

Never take away hope from
any human being.
—Oliver Wendell Holmes, Sr.

One thorn of experience is worth a whole
wilderness of warning.
—James Russell Lowell

Never wait for trouble.
—Charles "Chuck" Yeager

The time will come when winter will ask
what you were doing all summer.
—Henry Clay

You can't hold a man down without staying
down with him.
—Booker T. Washington

Conscience is the perfect interpreter of life.
—Karl Barth

If you tell the truth, you don't have
to remember anything.
—Mark Twain

Every charitable act is a stepping-stone
toward heaven.
—Henry Ward Beecher

Parenting with Patience

Parenting requires patience. From time to time, even the most mannerly children may do things that worry us, or confuse us, or anger us. Why? Because they are children and because they are human. And, it is precisely because they are human that we must, from time to time, be patient with our children's shortcomings (just as they, too, must be patient with ours). Sometimes, patience is the price we pay for being responsible parents, and that's as it should be. After all, think how patient our parents have been with us.

Patience and perseverance at length, accomplish more than anger or brute strength.

—

Jean de La Fontaine

Chapter 4
Courage

One man with
courage
is a majority.

—

Andrew Jackson

Thoughtful fathers teach the importance of courage and character, knowing that their children will then pass along the message to future generations. But, the teaching process requires more than words; morality lessons, like all paternal preachments, are best taught by example.

Heraclitus observed, "A man's fate is his character." He might have added that a father's character often contributes to the fate of his children. The following quotations remind us that character pays big dividends—now, and for generations to come.

Courage is the first of human qualities
because it is the quality which guarantees
all the others.
—Sir Winston Churchill

Courage is always the surest wisdom.
—Sir Wilfred Grenfell

When there is no money, half is gone;
when there is no courage, all is gone.
—Old Jewish Saying

Courage is grace under pressure.
—Ernest Hemingway

Nerve succeeds.

—Old Jewish Saying

Courage is contagious. When a brave man
takes a stand, the spines of others are
often stiffened.

—Billy Graham

When you're afraid, keep your mind
on what you have to do. And if you have
been thoroughly prepared,
you will not be afraid.

—Dale Carnegie

They conquer who believe they can.

—John Dryden

Character is that which can do without
success.
—Ralph Waldo Emerson

Character is what you are in the dark.
—Dwight L. Moody

Character is much easier kept than
recovered.
—Thomas Paine

Character is like the foundation of a house:
It lies beneath the surface and
everything else rests upon it.
—Anonymous

Even if fear can act as a good advisor,
there is no use cultivating it.
In the long run it can only hurt you.

—Luciano Pavarotti

Fear corrupts.

—John Steinbeck

Do the thing you fear and
the death of fear is certain.

—Ralph Waldo Emerson

Where is the university for courage?
The university for courage is to do
what you believe in!

—El Cordobés, world-renowned Spanish matador

Discontent is want of self-reliance.
—Ralph Waldo Emerson

We must have courage to bet on our ideas,
to take the calculated risk, and to act.
Everyday living requires courage if life
is to be effective and bring happiness.
—Maxwell Maltz

Courage is resistance to fear,
mastery of fear—not absence of fear.
—Mark Twain

The only courage that matters is the kind
that gets you from one moment to the next.
—Mignon McLaughlin

Parenting with Courage

Being a responsible father is, at times, a daunting task. Raising a family is never easy, but when times are tough, it can be downright frightening. When the storm clouds form overhead, we may find our faith stretched to the breaking point.

As fathers, we must, on occasion, feign courage even when we are afraid. Sometimes, even when we are worried or confused, we must follow the admonition of Robert Louis Stevenson who advised, "Share your courage with others, but keep your fears to yourself."

Are you trying to be a dedicated dad in a difficult world? You've got company. Fathers of this generation—and every one that preceded it—have faced the challenges and responsibilities of protecting and supporting their families. You face those same responsibilities; when you face them with character and courage, your family wins...and so do you.

You don't raise heroes,
you raise sons.
And if you treat them
like sons, they'll turn
out to be heroes,
even if it's just in
your own eyes.

—

Walter M. Schirra, Sr.

Chapter 5
Happiness

A good laugh is sunshine in a house.

—

William Makepeace Thackeray

Fathers seek happiness for their children but cannot force it upon them. Ultimately, each child must bear the responsibility for his own peace of mind—or lack thereof. As Aristotle observed, "Happiness depends upon ourselves."

While you, as a caring father, cannot force your children to be happy, you can prepare them for happiness by teaching them to live responsibly. If you earnestly desire happiness for your children, teach them discipline, optimism, generosity, honesty, self-reliance, courage, love, and faith. When you do, your children will discover happiness not because you gave it to them but because you taught them how to earn it for themselves.

Happiness comes of the capacity to
feel deeply, to enjoy simply, to think freely,
to risk life, to be needed.
—Storm Jameson

Happiness is when what you think,
what you say, and what you do
are in harmony.
—Mohandas Gandhi

Happiness is something you get as
a by-product in the process of making
something else.
—Aldous Huxley

Choose a job you love, and you will
never work a day in your life.
—Confucius

Mirth is better than fun, and happiness is
better than mirth.

—William Blake

Humor is the best therapy.

—Norman Cousins

An inexhaustible good nature is one
of the most precious gifts of heaven.

—Washington Irving

To live we must conquer incessantly;
we must have the courage to be happy.

—Henri Frédéric Amiel

I am happy and content because
            I think I am.
                              —Alain-René Lesage

Happiness is a habit. Cultivate it.
                              —Elbert Hubbard

Always laugh when you can; it is cheap
      medicine. Merriment is a philosophy
            not well understood.
      It is the sunny side of existence.
                              —George Gordon Byron

A man should so live that his happiness
      shall depend as little as possible
            on external things.
                              —Epictetus

Happiness depends, as Nature shows,
Less on exterior things than most suppose.

—William Cowper

The U.S. Constitution doesn't guarantee
happiness, only the pursuit of it.
You have to catch up with it yourself.

—Ben Franklin

Laughter has no foreign accent.

—Paul Lowney

To fill the hour and leave no crevice—that
is happiness.

—Ralph Waldo Emerson

Make the work interesting and
    the discipline will take care of itself.
                —E. B. White

Never is work without reward or
    reward without work.
                —Livy

I learned from my father how to work.
    I learned from him that work is life and
    life is work, and work is hard.
                —Philip Roth

Get happiness out of your work,
    or you may never know what happiness is.
                —Elbert Hubbard

Before we set our hearts too much on
   anything, let us examine how happy are
   those who already possess it.
   —La Rochefoucauld

He is the happiest, be he king or peasant,
   who finds peace in his home.
   —Goethe

Everyone chases after happiness,
   not noticing that happiness is at their heels.
   —Bertolt Brecht

The happiness of your life depends upon
   the character of your thoughts.
   —Marcus Aurelius

People with many interests live not only longest, but happiest.

—

George Matthew Adams

Encouraging Our Children

Think...pause...then speak: How wise is the father who can communicate in this way. But all too often, in the rush to have themselves heard, fathers may speak first and think later... with unfortunate results.

If we seek to be a source of encouragement to our children, we must measure our words carefully. Words, especially those spoken by a parent, have the power to hurt or to heal. Our words can uplift our children or discourage them. And, of course, if our words are reckless or spoken in haste, they cannot be erased.

As a loving father, your challenge is clear: You must choose words that encourage and empower your children. You must speak wisely, not impulsively. You must employ words of kindness and praise, not words of anger or derision. When you do, you will lift up your children today, and, more importantly, you will give them the confidence they need to lift themselves up tomorrow.

The best gift parents
can give children
is themselves.

—

Anonymous

Chapter 6
Faith

The greatest asset of
a man, a business,
or a nation, is faith.

—

Thomas J. Watson

Clement of Alexandria, the Greek theologian, observed, "Faith is the ear of the soul." He might have added that, when it comes to the spiritual ear, most of us suffer from occasional bouts of hearing loss. From time to time, we all fall prey to fits of depression, pessimism or doubt. Even fathers are not immune. But perceptive pops understand that when life gets tough, it's time to turn up the spiritual hearing aid.

No matter how big the problem, faith is the answer. Leo Tolstoy grasped this fact when he wrote, "Faith is the force of life." Hear, hear.

Faith can give us courage to face
the uncertainties of the future.
——Martin Luther King, Jr.

Faith is the daring of the soul to go farther
than it can see.
——William Newton Clark

When you enroll in the "school of faith,"
you never know what may happen next....
The life of faith presents challenges that
keep you going—and keep you growing!
——Warren Wiersbe

Treat the other man's faith gently;
it is all he has to believe with.
——Henry S. Haskins

Faith means being grasped by a power that
is greater than we are, a power that
shakes us and turns us, and transforms
and heals us. To surrender to this
power is faith.

—Paul Tillich

Faith is building on what you know is here,
so you can reach what you know is there.

—Cullen Hightower

All work that is worth anything is
done in faith.

—Albert Schweitzer

Belief is a truth held in the mind.
Faith is a fire in the heart.

—Joseph Fort Newton

Faith is required of thee, and a sincere life,
not loftiness of intellect, nor deepness in
the mysteries of God.

—Thomas à Kempis

Understanding is the reward of faith.
Therefore seek not to understand
that thou mayest believe, but believe that
thou mayest understand.

—St. Augustine

Faith is the substance of things hoped for,
the evidence of things not seen.

—Hebrews 11:1 KJV

Faith is a higher facility than reason.

—Philip James Bailey

Faith is reason grown courageous.

—Sherwood Eddy

Faith is knowing with your heart.

—N. Richard Nash

Hope is an adventure, a going forward—
a confident search for a rewarding life.

—Karl Menninger

Deep faith eliminates fear.

—Lech Walesa

Love is the seed of all hope.
It is the enticement to trust,
to risk, to try, to go on.

—Gloria Gaither

No faith is our own that we have
not arduously won.

—Havelock Ellis

No one is surprised over what God does
when he has faith in Him.

—Oswald Chambers

Entertain great hopes.

—Robert Frost

Hope deferred maketh the heart sick.

—Proverbs 13:12 KJV

Some things have to be believed to be seen.

—Ralph Hodgson

Faith for Today

When the sun is shining and all is well, it's easy to have faith. When the family is at peace, it is easy to feel at peace. When the pantry is full and the bank balance is high, it is easy to be optimistic. But, when life takes an unexpected turn for the worse, as it does on occasion, it is all too easy to lose faith in the future. To do so is a mistake of profound proportions.

During the darker days of life, we must never abandon faith; we must, instead, cultivate it. We must, without reservation, cultivate faith in ourselves, in our own abilities, and in our God. Then, armed with a faith that is grounded in reality but steeped in possibility, we can summon the courage to face our challenges head-on. When we do, we will be shocked at the power of mountain-moving faith.

And now, with no further ado, let the mountain moving begin.

They can conquer
who believe they can.

—

Ralph Waldo Emerson

Chapter 7
Hard Work

A journey
of a thousand miles
begins with one step.

—

Lao-tzu

The Book of Ecclesiasticus tells us that "Hard work is the lot of every man." It might be added that the lot of most fathers is very hard work. But, thoughtful dads don't just bring home the bacon; they teach their children to do the same.

Leonardo da Vinci observed, "God sells us all things at the price of labor." Hard-working fathers understand exactly what Leonardo meant: the key to success is a willingness to pay the price.

Savvy dads know that dreams become reality through the dint of hard work. And the time to get busy is now.

All work is as seed sown; it grows and
spreads and sows itself anew.

—Thomas Carlyle

The world is blessed most by men who
do things, and not by those who
merely talk about them.

—James Oliver

Everywhere in life, the true question
is not what we gain, but what we do.

—Thomas Carlyle

Make it a point to do something every day
that you don't want to do.
This is the golden rule for acquiring
the habit of doing your duty without pain.

—Mark Twain

The test of any man lies in action.

—Pindar

Life leaps like a geyser for those who drill
through the rock of inertia.

—Alexis Carrel

For purposes of action, nothing is more
useful than narrowness of thought
combined with energy of will.

—Henri Frédéric Amiel

He who considers too much will
perform little.

—Schiller

Knowing is not enough, we must apply;
willing is not enough, we must do.

—Goethe

The great end of life is not knowledge
but action.

—Thomas Huxley

Shallow men believe in luck.
Strong men believe in cause and effect.

—Ralph Waldo Emerson

Dreams pass into reality of action.
From the action stems the dream again;
and this interdependence
produces the highest form of living.

—Anaïs Nin

The world cares very little about what
a man or woman knows; it is what
the man or woman is able to do that counts.

—Booker T. Washington

Our main business is not to see what lies dimly at a distance, but to do what lies clearly at hand.

—Thomas Carlyle

Do noble things, do not dream them all day long.

—Charles Kingsley

Everything comes to him who hustles while he waits.

—Thomas Edison

To work is to pray.

—Benedictine Motto

If you can dream it, you can do it.

—Walt Disney

Do what you can with what you have
where you are.
—Theodore Roosevelt

Elbow grease is the best polish.
—English Proverb

Luck is the residue of design.
—Branch Rickey

You cannot plow a field by turning it
over in your mind.
—Anonymous

Do everything. One thing may
turn out right.
—Humphrey Bogart

Setting a Worthy Example

We live in a world that is filled to the brim with opportunities to make foolish choices. On the road of life, there exist countless dead ends, detours, and paths that lead far from the straight and narrow course. When we steer away from the path of prudence—and fall short by behaving foolishly or recklessly— we suffer (as do our families). But, when we, as concerned fathers, live honestly and wisely, we become powerful, enduring examples to our children.

The lessons that we teach our children come not from the words we speak but from the lives we live. May we live—and teach—accordingly.

Act well at the
moment, and you
have performed
a good action
for all eternity.
—

Johann K. Lavater

Trouble knocked at
the door but, hearing
a laugh within,
hurried away.

—

Poor Richard's Almanac

In the first century before the birth of Jesus, Publilius Syrus noted, "An angry father is most cruel toward himself." These words still apply. When a father loses his temper, he instantly becomes his own worst enemy. Unfortunately, the occasional pressures of fatherhood can make peace of mind an elusive goal, even for the most placid parent.

Peace of mind is a gift we give ourselves. The potential for happiness exists within us, but no force on earth can make us happy against our will. Therefore, questions concerning happiness are best posed to the man in the mirror; he is the man—the only man on earth—who can make us happy.

A thankful heart is not only the greatest
virtue, but the parent of all other virtues.

—Cicero

Thanksgiving invites God to bestow
a second benefit.

—Robert Herrick

In truth, to attain inner peace, one must be
willing to pass through the contrary to peace.

—Swami Brahmananda

Contentment is a pearl of great price,
and whoever procures it at the expense of
ten thousand desires makes a wise
and happy purchase.

—John Balguy

Order your soul; reduce your wants;
   live in charity; associate in Christian
   community; obey the laws;
   trust in Providence.
                              —St. Augustine

If there is to be any peace, it will come
   through being, not having.
                              —Henry Miller

Peace is not the absence of conflict,
   but the presence of God no matter
   what the conflict.
                              —Anonymous

Little minds have little worries.
   Big minds have no room for worries.
                              —Ralph Waldo Emerson

Better one hand full and peace of mind,
than both fists full and toil that is
chasing the wind.

—Ecclesiastes 4:6

I have learned, in whatever state I am,
therewith to be content.

—Philippians 4:11

Troubles are often the tools by which God
fashions us for better things.

—Henry Ward Beecher

There may be those on earth who dress
better or eat better, but those who enjoy
the peace of God sleep better.

—L. Thomas Holdcraft

The Joys and Frustrations of Fatherhood

Fatherhood is vastly rewarding, but, as every father knows, it can also be frustrating. No family is perfect, and even the most understanding dad's patience can wear thin on occasion.

When you are tempted to lose your temper over the minor inconveniences of family life, don't. Count to ten, and, if that doesn't work, keep counting. If you find yourself mired in the pit of negativity, take time for a much-needed pit stop. As you slow down to gather your emotions, turn your thoughts to the blessings and the love that have come and will come from the family that calls you "Dad." And how many blessings should you count? Count to ten, and, if that doesn't work, keep counting.

A man travels
the world over in
search of what
he needs and returns
home to find it.

—

George Moore

Chapter 9
Life

Life is 10% what you
make it and 90%
how you take it.

—

Irving Berlin

Henry James once advised, "Live all you can; it's a mistake not to. It doesn't so much matter what you do, so long as you have your life. If you haven't had that, what have you had?"

A father's job is to help his children understand that life should be savored, not squandered. It was Bishop Fulton J. Sheen who observed, "Time is so precious that God deals it out only second by second." This earthly life is, indeed, a brief interval between birth and death. Our challenge, of course, is to determine how best to use it...and to teach our children to do the same.

One life—a little gleam of time between
two eternities.

—Thomas Carlyle

Is not life a hundred times too short for us
to bore ourselves?

—Friedrich Nietzsche

There are two lasting bequests we can hope
to give our children. One of these is roots;
the other, wings.

—Hodding Carter

Real generosity toward the future consists
in giving all to what is present.

—Albert Camus

Life is what happens to us while we are
making other plans.

—Thomas La Mance

Everyone's life is a fairy tale written
by God's fingers.

—Hans Christian Andersen

Life is not a problem to be solved
but a reality to be experienced.

—Søren Kierkegaard

Life is like playing a violin in public
and learning the instrument as one goes on.

—Samuel Butler

Life is a series of collisions with the future;
it is not a sum of what we have been
but what we yearn to be.

—José Ortega y Gasset

Life is the art of drawing sufficient
conclusions from insufficient premises.
—Samuel Butler

Life is like a game of cards. The hand that
is dealt you represents determinism;
the way you play it is free will.
—Jawaharlal Nehru

The game of life is not so much in holding
a good hand as playing a poor hand well.
—H. T. Leslie

Our life is what our thoughts make it.
—Marcus Aurelius

Tell me whom you love, and
 I will tell you what you are.
                        —Arsène Houssaye

Life is a romantic business,
 but you have to make the romance.
                        —Oliver Wendell Holmes, Sr.

If you want to die happily, learn to live.
                        —Celio Calcagnini

Life is the flower of which love is the honey.
                        —Victor Hugo

Passion makes all things alive
 and significant.
                        —Ralph Waldo Emerson

The best way to
prepare for life
is to begin to live.

—

Elbert Hubbard

Celebrating Today

The 118th Psalm reminds us "This is the day which the Lord hath made; we will rejoice and be glad in it." As we rejoice in this day that the Lord has given, let us remember that an important part of today's celebration is the time we spend offering thanks. Each new dawn breaks upon a day filled with countless possibilities. To forget to say "Thank You" for these gifts is not simply poor manners, it is also sloppy thinking.

Today and every day therafter, let's give thanks for this opportunity called life. Even if the day holds a few unpleasant moments (as most days do), let us be thankful for the good times (which, for most of us, far outnumber the bad). Let's look for the good in others (starting with our families), and let us celebrate the good that we find. When we begin to search for reasons to celebrate the gift of life, we find them all around us...starting with those good people who live under the roof of the house we call home.

Thank God every morning when you get up that you have something to do that day which must be done, whether you like it or not.

—

Charles Kingsley

Chapter 10
Success

It takes twenty years
to make an overnight
success.
—
Eddie Cantor

P hillips Brooks observed, "To find his place and fill it is success for a man." But finding one's place is not always easy. Sometimes, a little fatherly advice can help.

The British writer George Bernard Shaw defined success by saying, "This is the true joy in life: being used for a purpose recognized by yourself as a mighty one." If you're interested in ways to recognize your place and successfully fill it, read on. The following quotations provide advice that any father would be proud to call his own.

The destiny of man is in his own soul.

—Herodotus

Success is simple. Do what's right,
the right way, at the right time.

—Arnold Glasow

Success abides longer among men
when it is planted by the hand of God.

—Pindar

He who would climb the ladder must
begin at the bottom.

—English Proverb

You always pass failure on the way
to success.

—Mickey Rooney

It takes time to be a good father.
It takes effort trying,
failing, and trying again.

—Tim Hansel

Being humble involves the willingness to
be reckoned a failure in everyone's sight
but God's.

—Roy M. Pearson

Success is to be measured not by wealth,
power, or fame, but by the ratio between
what a man is and what he might be.

—H. G. Wells

It is hard to fail, but it is worse never
to have tried to succeed.

—Theodore Roosevelt

Great minds have purposes,
        others have wishes.
           —Washington Irving

The man without a purpose is like a ship
        without a rudder—a waif,
        a nothing, a no man.
           —Thomas Carlyle

Try not to become a man of success
        but rather a man of value.
           —Albert Einstein

Life offers no assurances, so you might as
well do what you're really passionate about.
           —Jim Carrey

Whenever you see a successful business,
someone once made a courageous decision.
—Peter Drucker

Do your work with your whole heart,
and you will succeed—
there is so little competition.
—Elbert Hubbard

The secret of success is constancy
of purpose.
—Benjamin Disraeli

Einstein's three rules of work:
1. Out of clutter find simplicity.
2. From discord make harmony.
3. In the middle of difficulty lies
opportunity.

I look on that man as happy who,
   when there is question of success,
      looks to his work for a reply.
                              —Ralph Waldo Emerson

Success is relative. It is what we can make
   of the mess we have made of things.
                              —T. S. Eliot

Success has nothing to do with what you
   gain in life or accomplish for yourself.
      It is what you do for others.
                              —Danny Thomas

Living With a Purpose

Life is best lived on purpose. Unfortunately, too many of us begin each day without a clear idea of what we wish to accomplish...or why.

If you cannot lay your hands on a clear, concise version of your own personal mission statement, put down this book, grab a pen and paper, and start writing. Then, once you've clearly established what you wish to make of your life, get busy making it. And, while you're at it, teach your children to do likewise.

Human lives, like sailing ships, function best with maps and rudders. As you sail your own little ship on the seas of life, the map you use should be one of your own creation, and the rudder by which you steer should be placed firmly in the control of your own hand. Otherwise, you are not really sailing your own ship at all...you're simply cargo on someone else's boat. Resolve, therefore, to be the captain of your own vessel. And then, with your map in full view and your course clearly set, it's time to set sail... and live.

Success is finishing
what God gave
you to do.
—

Harold Cook

Chapter 11
Memories

It doesn't matter who my father was; it matters who I remember he was.

—

Anne Sexton

Memories of our fathers are price-
less possessions; in this chapter, a few notable
figures share theirs. Republican Howard Baker
once observed, "My father had a profound im-
pact on me in a way I don't think I could ever
explain." Democrat Mario Cuomo remembered
his father by saying, "I talk and talk and talk,
and I haven't taught people in 50 years what
my father taught by example in one week."
Mr. Baker and Mr. Cuomo thus proved once
and for all that admiration for our fathers is
something upon which even Republicans and
Democrats can agree.

Everyone had their chores. We all had to
eat together every meal. Mom cooked,
we helped, while we waited for Dad to
come home from work. It was like
the American Dream. My family was
almost perfect. I was very lucky.

—Reggie Miller

My father saved my life.

—Oprah Winfrey

The imprint of the parent remains forever
on the life of the child.

—C. B. Eavey

He was a gentleman and a gentle man.
My father was sweet, kind, and good-hearted.
He loved his family and spent
as much time as he could with us.

—Natalie Cole, on her father Nat King Cole

He gave me some valuable things:
he gave me fighting blood, which I needed.
—Tennessee Williams

My father was not a failure.
After all, he was the father
of a president of the United States.
—Harry S. Truman

I don't think I've been a particularly
good father, but I've been lucky in
the quality of my kids.
—Henry Fonda

When a child, my dreams rode on
your wishes, I was your son, high on your
horse, My mind atop whipped by the lashes
Of your rhetoric, windy of course.
—Stephen Foster

Pride in one's father reinforces love.

—

Margaret Truman

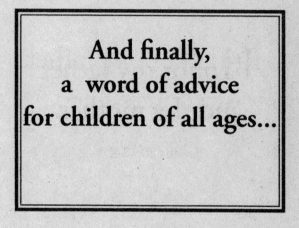

And finally,
a word of advice
for children of all ages...

Honor thy father and thy mother.

—

Exodus 20:12 KJV